WORLD BOOK
Reading Development Program

LEVEL 1 Book 1

World Book–Childcraft International, Inc.
A subsidiary of The Scott & Fetzer Company
Chicago London Sydney Tokyo Toronto

Printed in the United States of America

ISBN 0-7166-3123-7

STORIES

Pumpkin Race

Key Words
pumpkin
heavy

"Do you stop at Green Street?" Anita asked.

The bus driver said, "Yes, I do."

"Will you give my pumpkin a ride?" asked Anita. "It's too heavy. I can't ride my bike with it. I'll meet you at the Green Street bus stop."

The bus driver took the pumpkin.
He said, "Hurry. The bus won't wait."

The bus riders
smiled.

Anita got on her bike.
She zoomed off.
Her legs flashed
up and down,
up and down.

The bus riders
began yelling.

"Come on! Come on!"

"The bus won't
wait for me!"

"She will win!
Look at her go!"

“I’ll make it!”

The bus riders yelled.
"Hurray! You made it!"
"The winner!" Everyone clapped.

Anita took the pumpkin.
"Thank you," she said.
She waved.

The driver honked the horn.
The bus roared away.

The Race *supporting details*

Circle the right words.

1. Anita and the ____ had a race.
   a. bus b. car

2. The ____ watched the race.
   a. bus stop b. bus riders

3. Anita ____ the race.
   a. lost b. won

41 • Best score 3 • My score ....

How They Move *classification/outline*

Which things below have wheels? Put A before each. Put B before each thing with legs.

____ 1. Anita ____ 4. driver
____ 2. bus ____ 5. bus rider
____ 3. bike

129 • Best score 5 • My score ....

One Word Fits *vocabulary*

In each box, which word fits both blanks? Circle the word.

I'll meet you at the bus ____.
Do you ____ at Green Street?
a. fast b. stop

Will you give my pumpkin a ____?
I can't ____ my bike.
a. meet b. ride

1 • Best score 2 • My score 2
All Best Scores 10 • All My Scores 10

No Bus *prediction*

What do you think Anita would have done if no bus had come? What would you have done?

I woldint be Able to go ware I whated.

Key Words

camera
weather report
satellites
clouds

The Flying Camera

Will it rain tomorrow?
Should we take raincoats?
Turn on the TV.
Let's watch the weather report.
Then we will know.

But where does the weather
report come from?
Who tells the TV people?

Satellites tell them.
Satellites are like spaceships.
Satellites carry cameras.

Weather people send satellites into space. A satellite flies high above the clouds. Its camera takes pictures of the clouds.

The cloud pictures
show where there is rain.
They show where
there is sunshine.
They show which way
the wind blows.

Weather people read the
pictures and tell us if it
will rain or shine.

We can't see
tomorrow's
weather. But
satellites can.

Weather Report *sequence*

There is a 1 by the sentence that tells what happens first. Put 2, 3 and 4 by the other sentences to show when they happen.

_____ We watch the weather report.
_____ Weather people read pictures.
__1__ Satellites are sent into space.
_____ Satellites take pictures.

105 • Best score 4 • My score ....

Satellites *inferences*

Check (✓) three true sentences.

_____ 1. Satellites can make rain.
_____ 2. Satellites tell about weather.
_____ 3. Satellites fly very high.
_____ 4. Satellites are helpful.

65 • Best score 3 • My score ....

Weather Words *vocabulary*

Use the words below to fill in the blanks.

a. cameras
b. spaceships
c. rain

1. Weather satellites carry ___a___.

2. Satellites are like ___b___.

3. Cloud pictures may show where ___c___ can be found.

49 • Best score 3 • My score ....3....
All Best Scores 10 • All My Scores ....10....

Turn It On! *prediction*

How does the weather report help us?

In what other ways might flying cameras help us?

take Pictchers of clouds.

Key Words
desert
body
often
lashes

The Camel

Look at the camel.
It looks funny!

See the hump on its back?
See its strange face? See its thin legs?

The camel needs these funny body parts. It lives in the desert. It works very hard.

The desert is hot and dry. Most animals need a lot of water. But the camel doesn't stop for water very often. It can keep water in its body for many days.

Long lashes keep sand out of the camel's eyes. When strong winds blow, the lashes drop down.

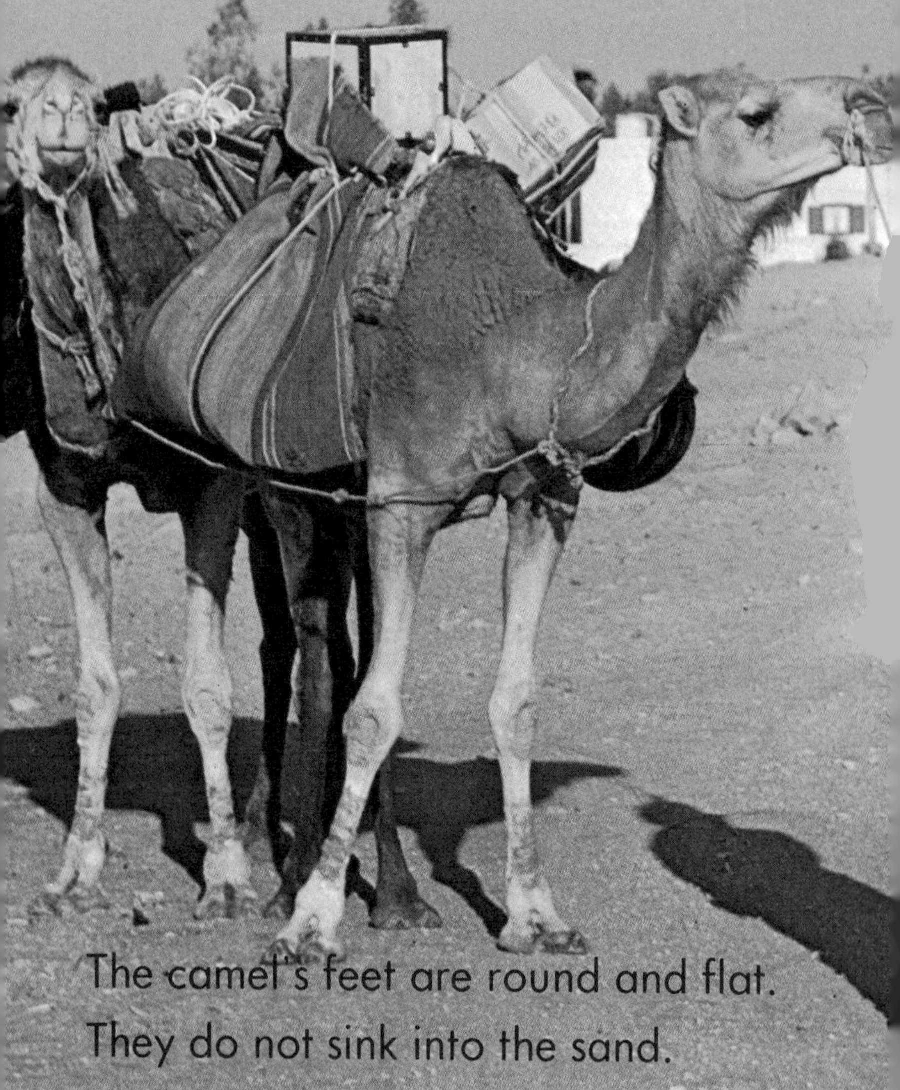

The camel's feet are round and flat. They do not sink into the sand.

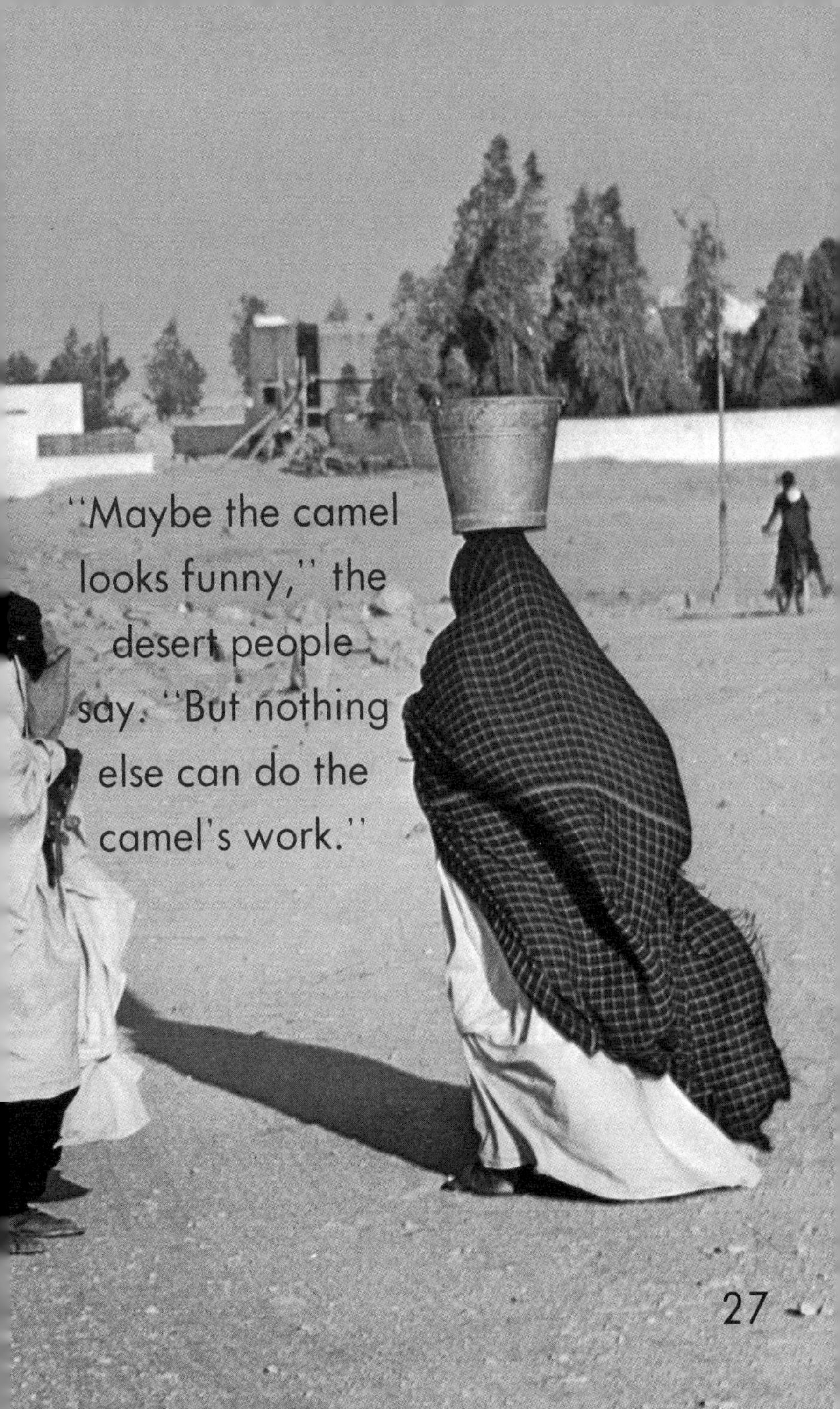

"Maybe the camel looks funny," the desert people say. "But nothing else can do the camel's work."

A Talking Camel *supporting details*

Pretend the camel is talking. Circle the right words.

1. I live in the ____.
   a. desert   b. sea

2. I can keep water in my ____.
   a. body   b. nose

3. My ____ help me walk on sand.
   a. teeth   b. flat feet

4. My ____ keep sand out of my eyes.
   a. humps   b. lashes

86 • Best score 4 • My score ....

About the Desert *classification/outline*

Circle three desert words.

1. wet   3. dry
2. sandy   4. hot

65 • Best score 3 • My score ....

Same Meaning *sentence meaning*

Desert people say, "Nothing else can do the camel's work." Circle three other things the desert people might say.

1. We can't use trucks on sand.

2. We can ride the camel for days without stopping for water.

3. We do not like camels.

4. We need camels.

66 • Best score 3 • My score ....

All Best Scores 10 • All My Scores ....

On Your Trip *prediction*

Make believe you are going to a desert. What would you take? What would you do in the desert? How long would you stay?

The Bus Stop

Key Words
fire hydrant

Rain splashed on Ricky's yellow hat.
Plop, plop, plop!

Rain rolled down his yellow coat.

Drip, drip, drip.

Rain fell on his yellow boots.

Splush!

Ricky stood at the bus stop.

The bus drove up. The door did not open. The driver sat and sat and sat. She did not open the door.

Ricky stood still.

He waited and waited.

The door did not open.

Honk! Honk! blew the horn.

Honk! Honk!

Ricky jumped at the sound. Then the door popped open.

"Is that you, Ricky?" the driver asked. "I thought you were a fire hydrant."

Name Game *main idea*

This story is called "The Bus Stop." Check (✓) two other names that tell about the story.

____ 1. The Fire Truck
____ 2. Ricky Waits in the Rain
____ 3. The Fire Hydrant

12 • Best score 2 • My score ....

It's Ricky! *cause/effect*

Why did the bus driver think Ricky was a fire hydrant? Check (✓) three answers.

____ 1. The bus was late.
____ 2. Rain made Ricky hard to see.
____ 3. Ricky had yellow clothes.
____ 4. Ricky looked the same size as a fire hydrant.

65 • Best score 3 • My score ....

Look in the Story *skimming*

Look in the story for the words in each list. Check (✓) the words you find.

Ricky's Clothes

✓ 1. coat

___ 2. shoes

✓ 3. hat

✓ 4. boots

Parts of a Bus

✓ 5. horn

✓ 6. door

___ 7. window

🔑 168 • Best score 5 • My score ....

All Best Scores 10 • All My Scores ....

Listen to Words *figurative language*

Which words in the story help you hear sounds? Say other sound words.

Key Words

lookout
whole
tower
ranger
lonely
write

On Top of the World

"Guess what!" Miss Wills told her class. "This summer I'll sit on top of the world!"

The class laughed. "How will you do that?" asked Kim.

"It's my summer job," Miss Wills said. "I'll be a forest lookout."

"Oh," Carlos said. "I know what that means. You will watch out for fires."

"How can you watch a whole forest?"asked Maria.

"I'll work in a tower," said Miss Wills. "Each morning I'll climb up. I'll work in a small room at the top. At night I'll live in a house near the tower."

"What if you see smoke?" asked Lisa.

"I'll radio a forest ranger," said Miss Wills. "He will know what to do."

"Will you make a lot of money?" asked Harry.

"No, I won't," Miss Wills told him. "But think how pretty the woods are. It will be a good summer!"

"Won't you be lonely?" asked Pat.

"Not if you write to me," Miss Wills said.

"We will," the class sang out.

"Good," Miss Wills said. "I'll write to you, too. I'll tell you how it feels to be on top of the world."

What Miss Wills Said *sequence*

Put 1 next to what happened first.
Put 2 next to what happened next.
Put 3 next to what happened last.

__3__ Miss Wills said that she will write to the class.

__2__ Miss Wills said it would be a good summer.

__1__ Miss Wills said that she will have a summer job.

54 · Best score 3 · My score.........

Miss Wills *characterization*

Circle five words that tell about Miss Wills.

1. kind
2. friendly
3. happy
4. nice
5. lonely
6. good

169 · Best score 5 · My score.........

Make It Right *cause/effect*

Circle the word that makes each sentence right.

1. If Miss Wills sees smoke, she will know there is a _____ in the forest.

   a. fire b. lookout

2. Miss Wills won't be lonely because the class will _____ to her.

   a. call b. write

2 • Best score 2 • My score.........

All Best Scores 10 • All My Scores.........

Name the Story *main idea*

Why do you think this story is named "On Top of the World"?

Why is that a good name? Think of some other names that tell about the story.

Let's Hear It!

Key Words
someone
phone
drum
bones
sounds
messages
brain

You have two of them. You can't make them move much. But you use them all the time. You even use them when you sleep.

Do you know what they are?
They are your ears. You use
them in many ways.

You hear running feet.
Someone calls, "Wait for me!"
You know it's your friend. Your
ears help to tell you.

You are asleep. A bell wakes you up. You know the phone is ringing. Your ears tell you.

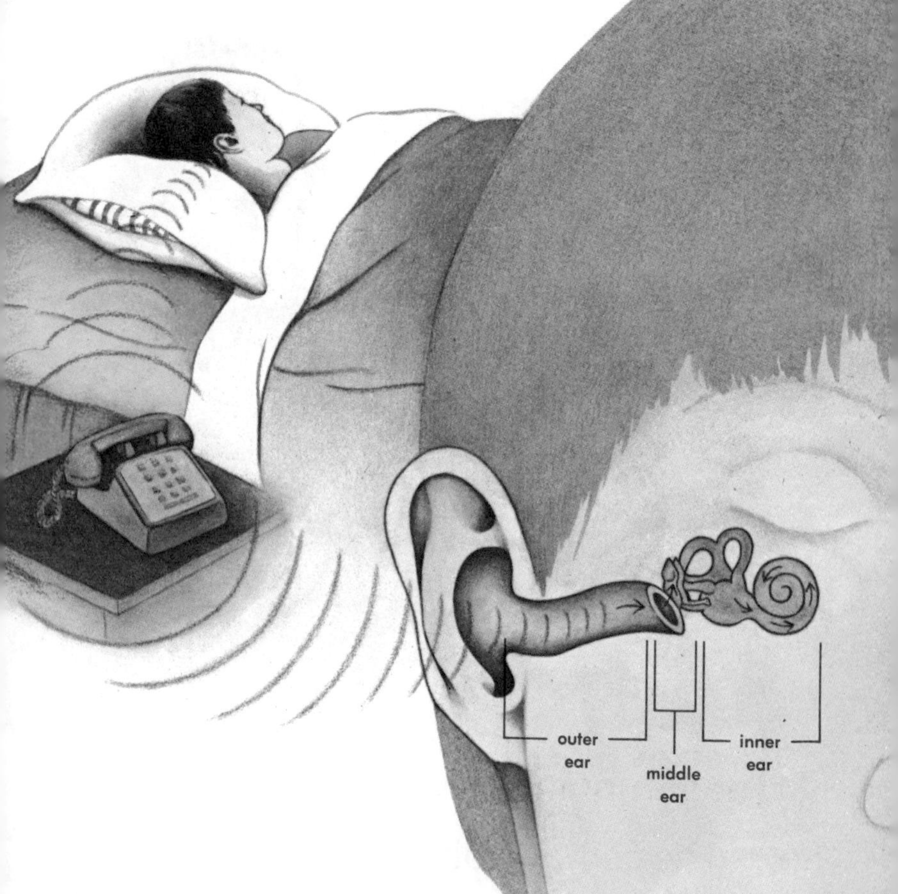

Many tiny parts make your ears work. Inside each ear is a

part like a tiny drum. And in back of the drum are three tiny bones.

What beats on the drum? Sounds do! Sounds in the air hit the drum. They make the drum move a little.

The drum moves the three tiny bones. And the moving bones send messages to your brain. Then you hear.

Your brain tells you what the sound is. It lets you know what to do. Then you answer the phone. Or you stop and say "Hi" to your friend.

What Do You Hear? *sequence*

There is a 1 by the sentence that tells what happened first. Put 2, 3, and 4 by the other sentences to show when they happen.

____ You hear the bell.
____ The drum wiggles three tiny bones.
__1__ A bell makes a sound.
____ Sounds in the air hit the drum.

105 · Best score 4 · My score........

Your Ears *inferences*

Check (✔) two true sentences.

____ 1. Your ears don't help you much.
____ 2. A tiny drum is inside each of your ears.
____ 3. Your brain tells you what you hear.

12 · Best score 2 · My score........

Hear This *supporting details*

Circle the right words.

1. You use your ____ in many ways.
   a. ears   b. eyes
2. Inside each ear is a tiny ____.
   a. bell   b. drum
3. ____ make the drum wiggle.
   a. Sounds   b. Winds
4. The drum wiggles ____ tiny bones in your ear.
   a. two   b. three

🗝 84 · Best score 4 · My score.........

All Best Scores 10 · All My Scores.........

Sounds *classification/outline*

Fold a piece of paper in two. Write Loud Sounds on one part and Soft Sounds on the other part. Draw a picture of each thing on the right part of the paper.

a big drum L   a kitten S   an airplane L
a dump truck L   a bird S   a small bell S

Key Words
snowflakes
draw
catch
count

Snow Stars

Can you catch a star? Yes, you can. You can catch snow stars.

Snowflakes have snow stars in them. Catch some snowflakes and look!

Here are some pictures of snow stars. How pretty the stars are!

These pictures were taken on a cold day. The snow stars were very small. In the pictures, they look big.

No two snow stars are just the same. But every snow star has six arms. Count them and see!

Snow stars are made of water. They are made high in the sky.

Down here, the little stars melt fast. You must look fast to see them.

You can't keep snow stars. But you can keep pictures of them.

Wait until snow falls. Then catch some snowflakes on a dark coat.

Each snowflake may have many snow stars in it. Look at the stars. Which one do you like best? Try to draw its picture.

The star will melt fast. So, be quick!

Tell the Story *story elements*

Put the letter of the word that belongs in each sentence.

a. sky c. water
b. arms d. snowflake

1. A snow star has six ______.
2. Snow stars are made of ______.
3. There are many snow stars in a ______.
4. Snow stars are made in the ______.

103 · Best score 4 · My score.........

A Winter Day *classification/outline*

Circle three words that tell about a winter day.

1. cold 3. hot
2. snowy 4. chilly

66 · Best score 3 · My score.........

Snow Stars *summary*

Check (✓) three things that tell about snow stars.

____ 1. Snow stars are big.
__✓__ 2. Snowflakes are made of snow stars.
__✓__ 3. Snow stars are made of water.
__✓__ 4. Snow stars will melt fast.
____ 5. All snow stars are just the same.

🗝65 · Best score 3 · My score.........

All Best Scores 10 · All My Scores.........

How Things Feel *comparison/contrast*

Snowflakes are cold.
Name other things that feel cold.
Name things that feel these ways.

hot soft hard wet dry

Look! It's an Animal!

Key Words
markings
slinks
pounces
enemy

Can you see the tiger? Its markings look like the grass. The tiger can hide in the grass.

Markings help the tiger catch other animals. The tiger slinks near an animal. The animal can't see the tiger. The tiger pounces!

This bird hides in the leaves. The bird sits very still. An enemy can't see it. The bird is safe.

Many animals live in places that look like the animals' markings.

Look closely at a tree or bush. You might see an animal.

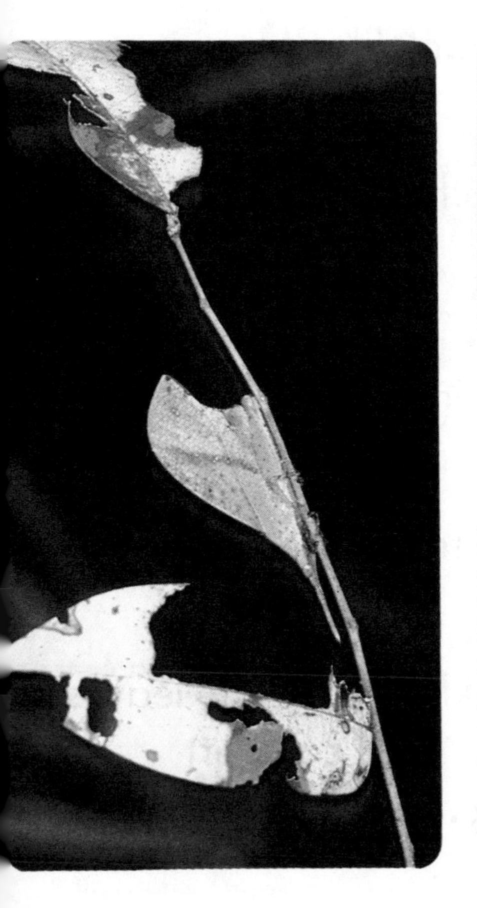

Animals in the Story *supporting details*

Circle the word or words that make each sentence right.

1. ____ help the tiger hide.
   a. Markings b. Eyes

2. The markings look like the ____.
   a. enemy b. grass

3. Markings help the tiger catch other ____.
   a. grass b. animals

4. The bird hides in the ____.
   a. cage b. leaves

5. The bird hides from its ____.
   a. friend b. enemy

6. The bird's markings ____ the leaves.
   a. look like b. can hurt

174 • Best score 6 • My score ....

Go Together *classification/outline*

In each box, which word does not belong? Put an X on the word.

1. bird 2. cup 3. tiger	1. animals 2. grass 3. leaves
1. colors 2. slinks 3. pounces	1. colors 2. words 3. markings

88 • Best score 4 • My score ....

All Best Scores 10 • All My Scores ....

Hiding Places *graphics*

Look at the pictures on page 63. Can you find a bug, rabbit and bird? How do markings help each animal hide?

Steel Bands

Key Words
island
Trinidad
steel
drums
dents

On the island of Trinidad, people make music with old cans!

The cans are very wide and deep. They are made of steel.

These big cans are called drums. When the drums are empty, people throw them away.

But a man of Trinidad found out how to make music on a steel drum. Here is how he did it.

This man made dents on the top of an old steel drum. Then he tapped a dent. He got a sound. And each dent made a different sound.

The sounds were not loud bangs. They were soft, pretty sounds. They were like the sounds of bells.

The man learned to play tunes
by tapping different dents.
Other people heard him play.
Everyone liked the sound of
his music.

Soon, many
people learned
to play music
on steel drums.

Today, there are many steel bands in Trinidad. People who go there like to hear the soft, pretty music of the steel bands.

The Busy Man *sentence meaning*

The man in the story did many things. Circle four sentences that tell what the man did.

1. He made dents on a steel drum.
2. He tapped on the dents.
3. He made different sounds.
4. He played a horn.
5. He learned to play tunes.

117 · Best score 4 · My score ....

About the Story *generalizations*

Circle two true sentences.

1. There are no more steel bands.
2. Steel drums can make music.
3. Steel bands began in Trinidad.

12 · Best score 2 · My score ....

New Words *vocabulary*

Circle the right word.

1. Steel _____ began in Trinidad.
   a. bands   b. buildings

2. The man made _____ in the top of the drum.
   a. dents   b. cakes

3. The man tapped the drum on the _____.
   a. side   b. top

4. The drum made a _____ sound.
   a. loud   b. pretty

🔑 86 · Best score 4 · My score ....

All Best Scores 10 · All My Scores ....

Bands *classification/outline*

What kinds of bands do you like?

I Miss the Steam Whistle

Key Words
steam
whistle
whiz

New trains whiz
down the tracks.
Their horns toot.
But trains have changed.
New trains don't have
steam whistles.

I loved the old train's steam whistle.
It had a nice sound.

When it blew, it made me wonder—
"Where is the train coming
from? Where is it going?"

Sometimes the whistle seemed to say—
Jump on! Let's go far away!

Most of the time, the whistle made me feel good inside. Whoo-a-whoo. Whoo-a-whoo. This told me—
All is well. All is well.

Sounds and Thoughts *summary*

Steam whistles made the writer think five things. Circle each.

1. All is well!
2. Stop that sound!
3. Where is it coming from?
4. Where is it going?
5. Jump on!
6. Let's go far away!

168 • Best score 5 • My score ....

Sounds and Feelings *author's purpose*

How did the writer feel about steam whistles? Circle two pictures that show you.

a  b  c 

9 • Best score 2 • My score ....

The Writer *inferences*

1. About how old is the writer? Circle the picture that shows you.

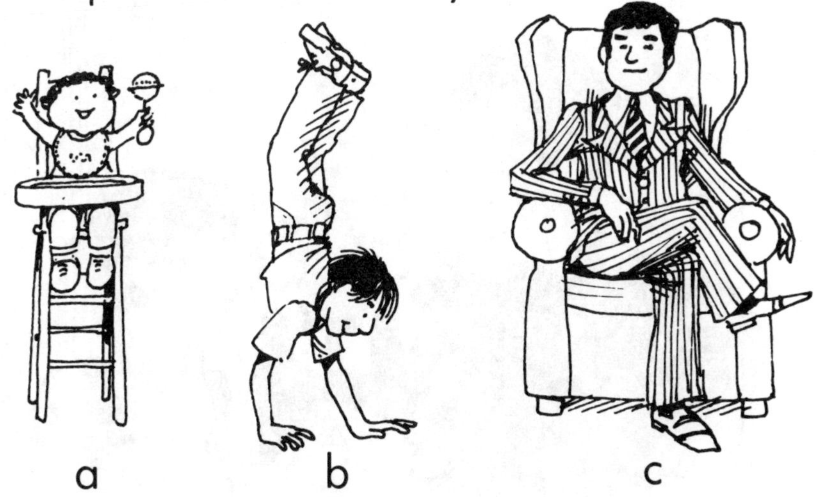

2. Circle two things the writer heard.
   a. horns   b. whistles   c. drums

16 • Best score 3 • My score ....

All Best Scores 10 • All My Scores ....

Think Back *analogy*

Do you miss something you had when you were younger? What was it?

Key Words
sew, sewed
cloth

The Toy Maker

Everyone in town liked Mrs. Steiff. They all called her Aunt Margaret. She could laugh and play. She could read and sing. But she could not walk.

Aunt Margaret wanted a job. What could she do?

"I can sew," she said. "I don't have to walk to do that."

Aunt Margaret cut some cloth.
She sewed the pieces. Then she
smiled. She had made a toy elephant.

Children loved the toy.
They shouted—
"Make me one, Aunt Margaret."
"Please! Please!"
"Make mine with pink spots."

Aunt Margaret smiled.
"You will all have toys."
She snipped and sewed,
snipped and sewed.

Soon Aunt Margaret had a zoo.
She made yellow chickens,
squirrels, tigers and
soft kittens.

Children in other towns soon
wanted toy animals. Aunt Margaret
started a toy shop. She made
lots of animals to sell.

Aunt Margaret worked hard.
Many people worked in her shop.
Her animals were sold
in many towns.

One day Aunt Margaret made a surprise. It was a fuzzy brown animal. It had black button eyes. Its arms and legs moved. Aunt Margaret called it Bear.

Many people say this was the first Teddy Bear. It became the most loved animal of all.

Aunt Margaret *supporting details*

Which sentences tell about Aunt Margaret? Draw a line under three.

1. She could not walk.
2. She made toy animals.
3. Children loved her.
4. She worked on a farm.

55 • Best score 3 • My score ....

The Toy Shop *graphics*

What would you find in Aunt Margaret's shop? Circle three things.

62 • Best score 3 • My score ....

As She Worked *characterization*

What might Aunt Margaret say? Draw a line under four things.

1. "I love children."
2. "I like my job."
3. "I want people to be happy."
4. "I am always sad."
5. "Toys are fun."
6. "I drive a bus."
7. "I make just one kind of toy animal."

🗝 117 • Best score 4 • My score ....

All Best Scores 10 • All My Scores ....

Snip and Sew *inferences*

Did Aunt Margaret work hard? How do you know?

What do you like about Aunt Margaret?

Key Words
hockey
ushers
ready
fans
cheers

Before the Game Starts

"May I feel the ice?" Amy asked.
"I have never seen it close up."

Amy and her father were
standing by an ice floor.
They were inside a big building.

Amy looked around.
She said, "I have seen
many things here. But
I like ice hockey games best."

"I like working here,"
Amy's father said. "I'm glad
you came with me today."

"The game is not until tonight,"
said Amy. "What can you
do now?"

Her father smiled.
"There's lots of work."

He was right. Many people were working very hard. Some dusted seats. Some swept floors. Some cooked hot dogs.

One man went downstairs. He started the ice-maker.
It would keep the ice floor very cold during the game.

Later more workers came. Food sellers stuffed their boxes with popcorn, peanuts and candy. Many ushers stood by the doors. They were ready to help the fans find seats.

Soon the fans came.
The game began.
Cheers filled the building.

The cheers did
not stop until the
game ended.

Then the fans went home. Only the workers stayed to clean up.

"The building is quiet again," Amy thought. "It is left to the people who love it best."

From Amy's Seat *main idea*

What did Amy learn? Draw a line under two sentences.

1. Many things are done before a hockey game.
2. Many people work at the hockey game.
3. The workers leave before the fans.
4. It is easy to play ice hockey.

🗝 7 • Best score 2 • My score ....

One Word—Two Meanings *vocabulary*

Make an X on two pictures of fans.

🗝 12 • Best score 2 • My score ....

Hockey Talk *points of view*

Who might say each thing?
Pick from these people.

1. Amy
2. food seller
3. usher
4. cook
5. fans
6. Amy's dad

Who . . .	Might Say This?
6	"I brought Amy to the game
2	"Peanuts for sale!"
3	"I'll help you find a seat."
4	"I made 100 hot dogs."
1	"My dad works here."
5	"Let's cheer for our team."

211 • Best score 6 • My score ....
All Best Scores 10 • All My Scores ....

A Special Place *comparison/contrast*

Which do you like better: a busy place or a quiet place? Why?